Alphabet of Bible Creatures

Considering God in His Creation

by Peggy Noll

Illustrations by Cheryl DeGraaf

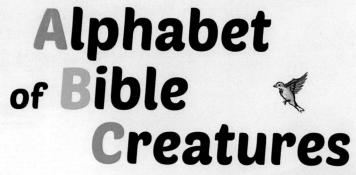

giraffe
& vole
press

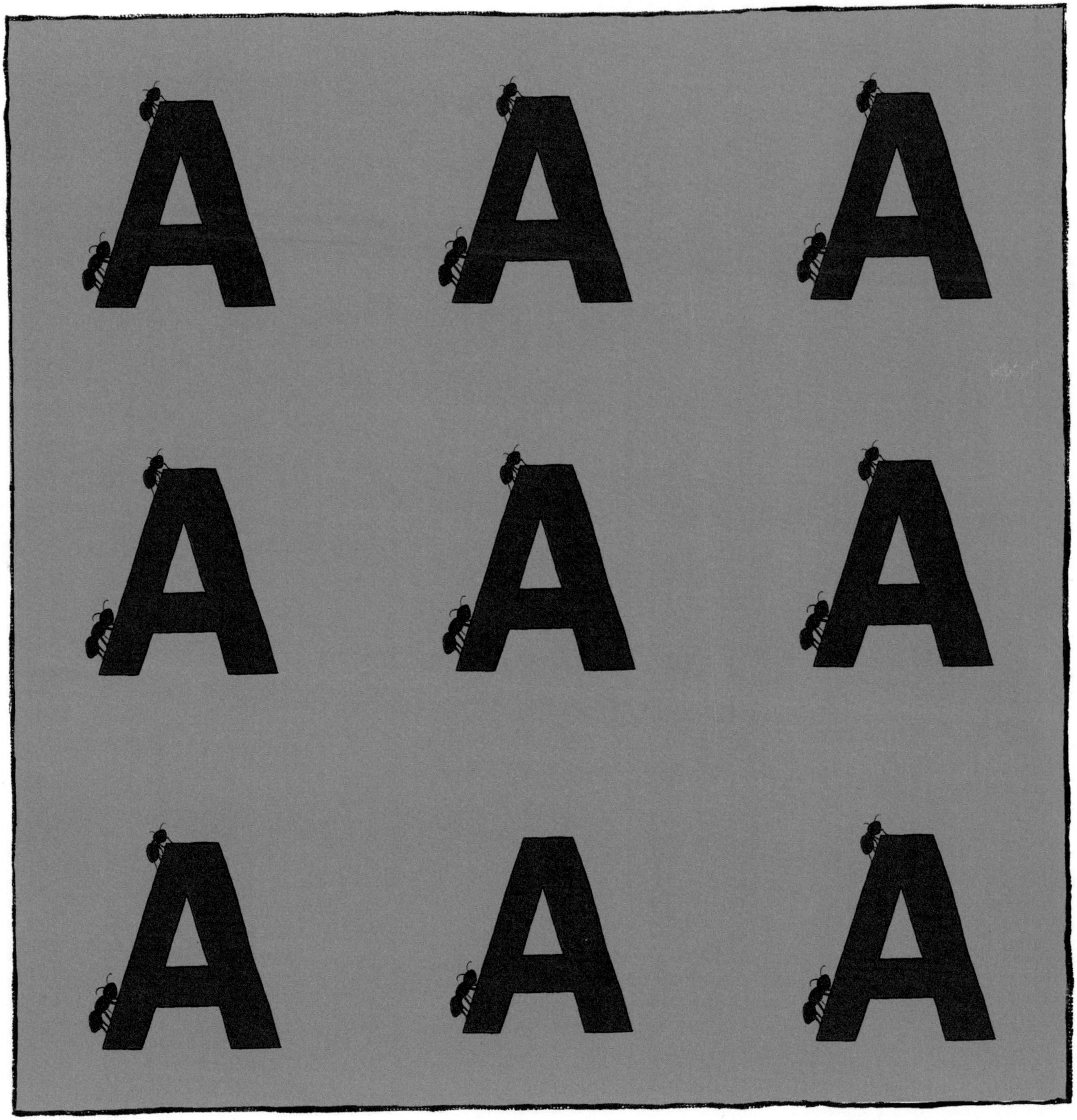
A
A
A
A
A
A
A
A
A

The ant with a big crumb of bread
Found friends to help haul it ahead.
Her hard-working ways
Have earned her God's praise:
"Be wise and consider her ways."

A
ant

Go to the ant, O sluggard;
consider her ways, and be wise.
-Proverbs 6:6

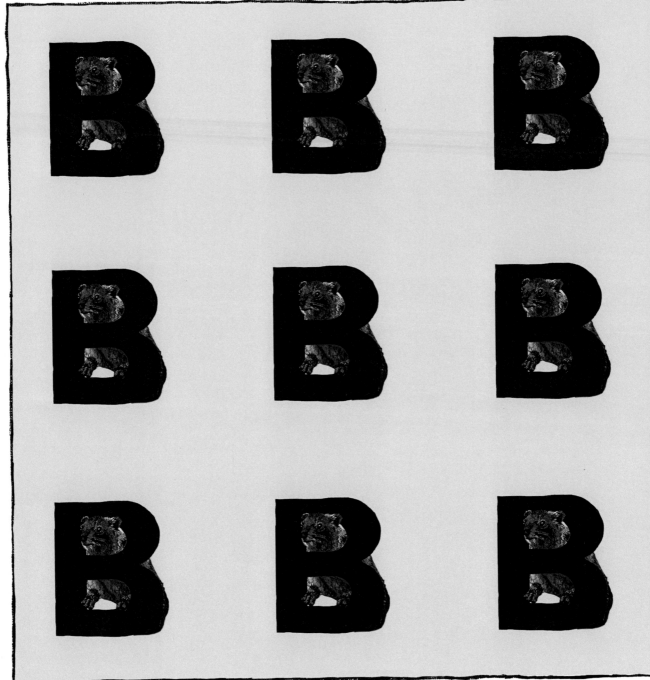

When **badgers** are hiding in homes underground,
Rocks are the refuge where they may be found.
When we are afraid or in danger from men,
God is our rock and our refuge and friend.

badger

The rocks are a refuge for the rock badgers. -Psalm 104:18
My God, my rock, in whom I take refuge. -Psalm 18:2

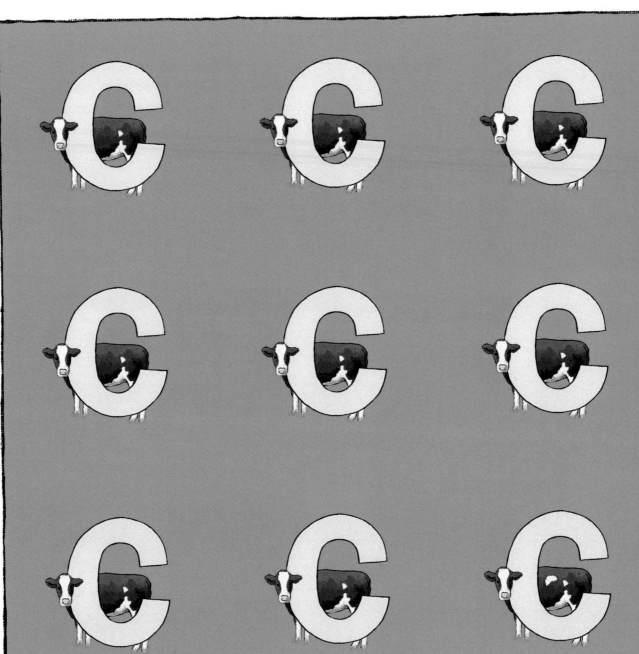

The cattle on a thousand hills

Peacefully are grazing.

Above their heads God's mighty sun

Everywhere is blazing.

For every beast of the forest is mine, the cattle on a thousand hills.
-Psalm 50:10

cattle

From the rising of the sun to its setting, the name of the LORD is to be praised!
-Psalm 113:3

Balaam's donkey on the path
Saw the angel of the Lord.
By obeying God, not man,
He saved his master
from the sword.

donkey

And the donkey saw the angel of the LORD standing in the road, with a drawn sword in his hand... -Numbers 22:23

We must obey God rather than men. -Acts 5:29

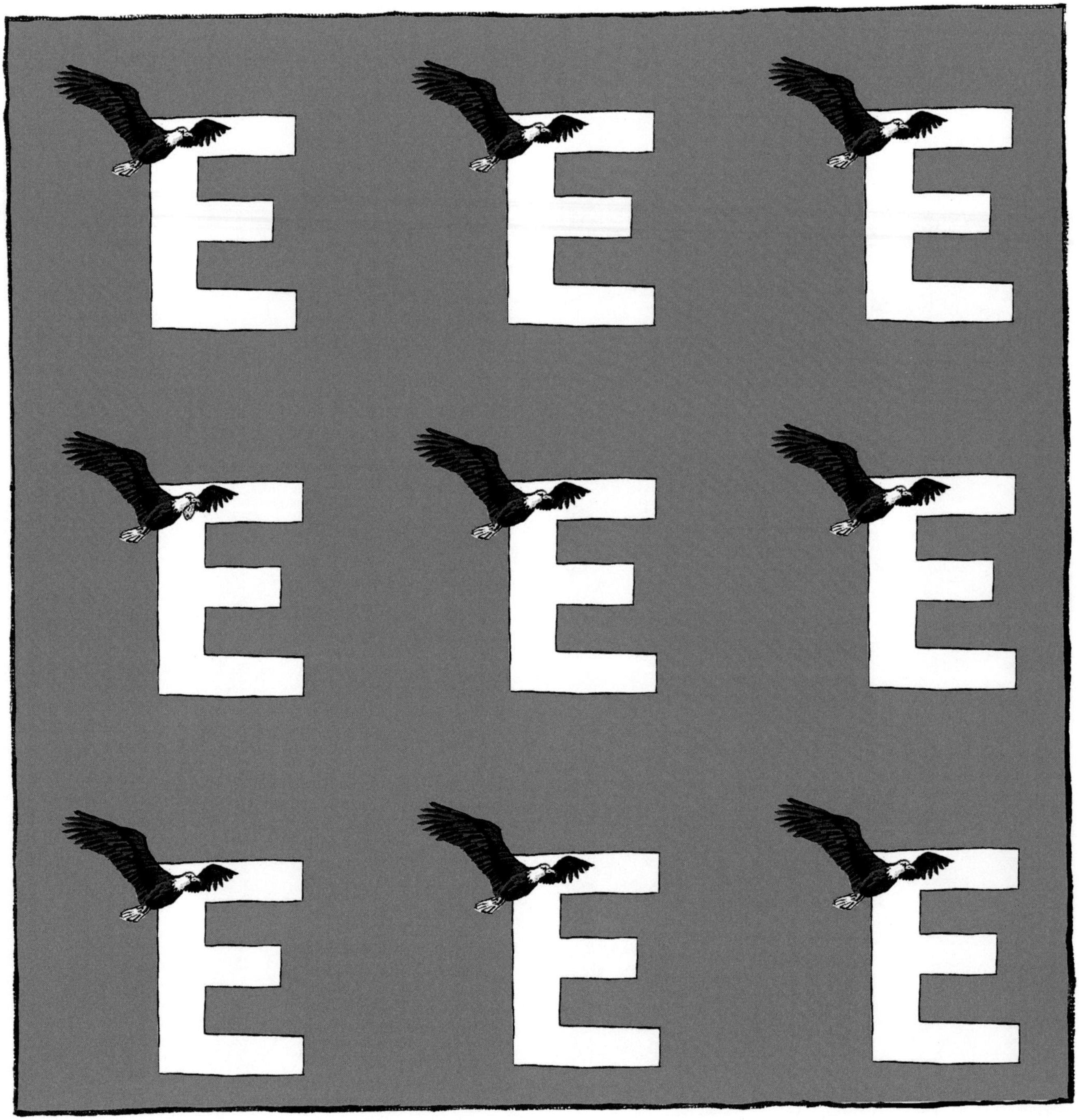
E E E
E E E
E E E

eagle

An **eagle** is soaring between two peaks,
Swooping to locate the nest that
    it seeks.
Isaiah the prophet
    the **eagle's** flight sees--
A picture of hope bringing
    strength to weak knees.

But they who wait for the LORD shall renew their strength;
they shall mount up with wings like eagles. -Isaiah 40:31

Frogs **jumped here,** frogs **jumped there,**
Frogs **kept hopping everywhere.**
Frogs **hid under Pharoah's bed,**
Frogs **leaped onto Pharoah's head.**
Pharoah still insisted, "No!"
"I will not let those Hebrews go."

frog

...and the frogs came up and covered the land of Egypt... But Pharoah hardened his heart and would not listen. -Exodus 8:6,15

The way of a fool is right in his own eyes, but a wise man listens to advice.
-Proverbs 12:15

Goats go to one side,
Sheep to the other.
Christ is the true judge
Of us—and our brother!

G goat

When the Son of Man comes in his glory, and all the angels with him, then he will sit on his glorious throne. Before him will be gathered all the nations, and he will separate people one from another as a shepherd separates the sheep from the goats.
-Matthew 25:31-32
God is a righteous judge.
-Psalm 7:11

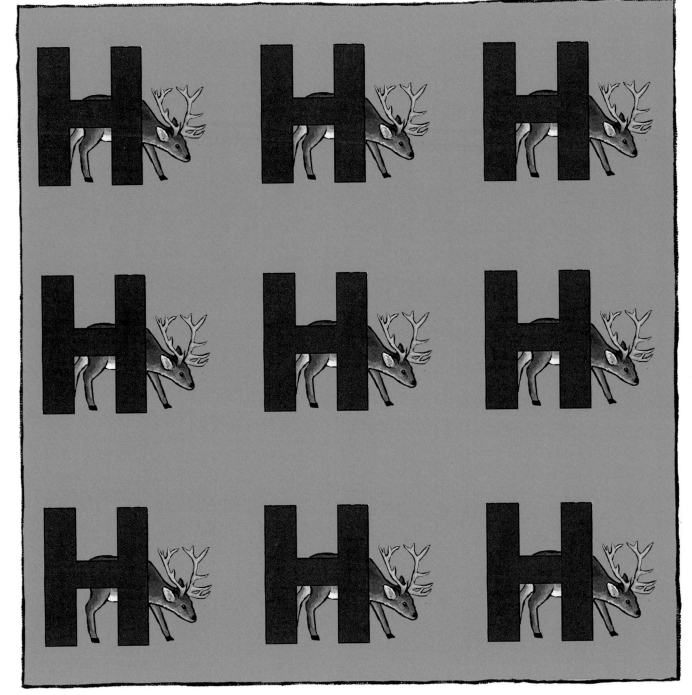

A **hart** seeks after
    flowing streams—
Is this our **heart**'s thirst, too?
A desperate search for God alone,
Whose Spirit makes us new.

hart

As the hart panteth after the water brooks, so panteth my soul after thee, O God. -Psalm 42:1 KJV

If anyone thirsts, let him come to me and drink. *Whoever believes in me, as the Scripture has said, 'Out of his heart will flow rivers of living water.' Now this he said about the Spirit...* -John 7:37-39

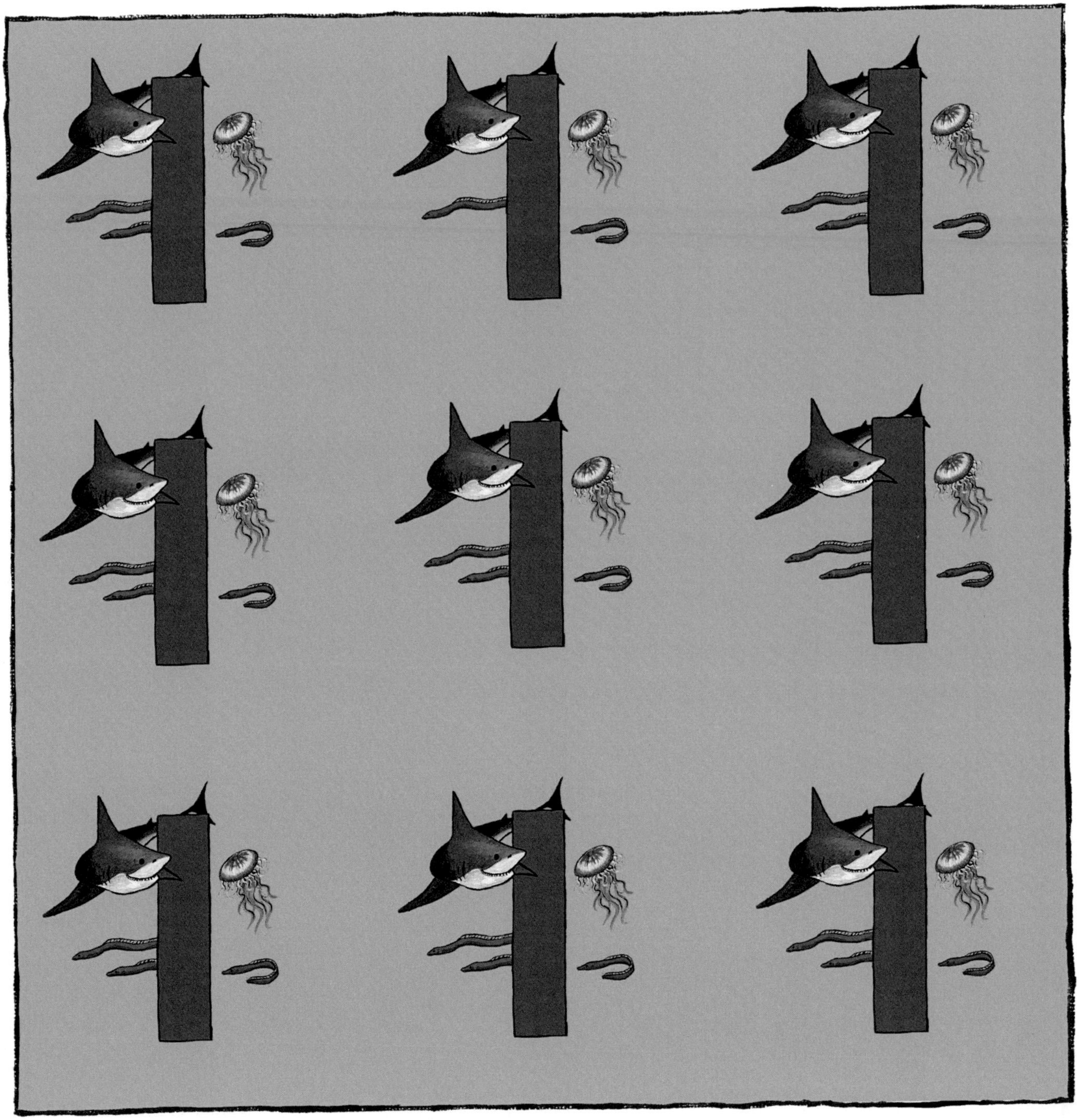

Innumerable are the species
That glide beneath the seas.
The eels, the whales, the great white sharks—
God takes delight in these.

innumerable

O Lord, how manifold are your works!
In wisdom you have made them all;
Here is the sea, great and wide,
Which teems with creatures innumerable... -Psalm 104:24-25

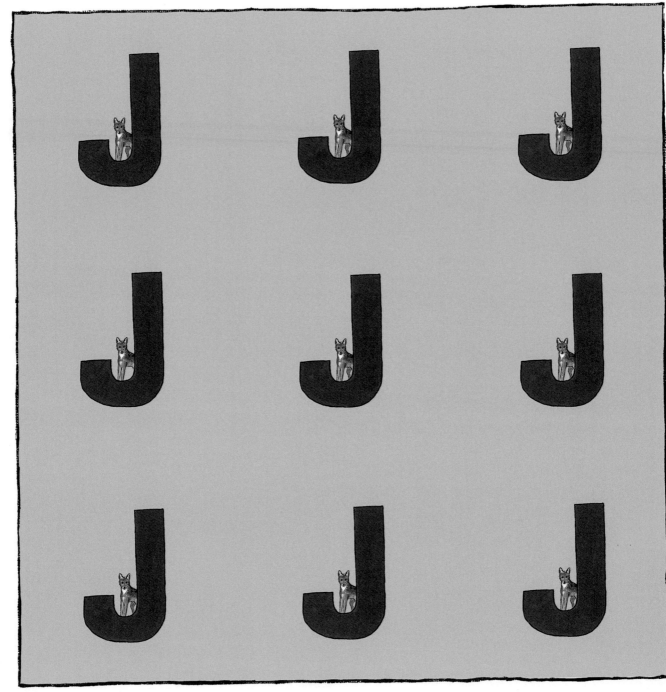

Jackals were outsiders—
Job was in despair
When he called them brothers.
Where was God, O where?

jackal

I am a brother of jackals and
a companion of ostriches.
-Job 30:29

The LORD gave and the LORD
has taken away; blessed be
the name of the LORD. -Job 1:21

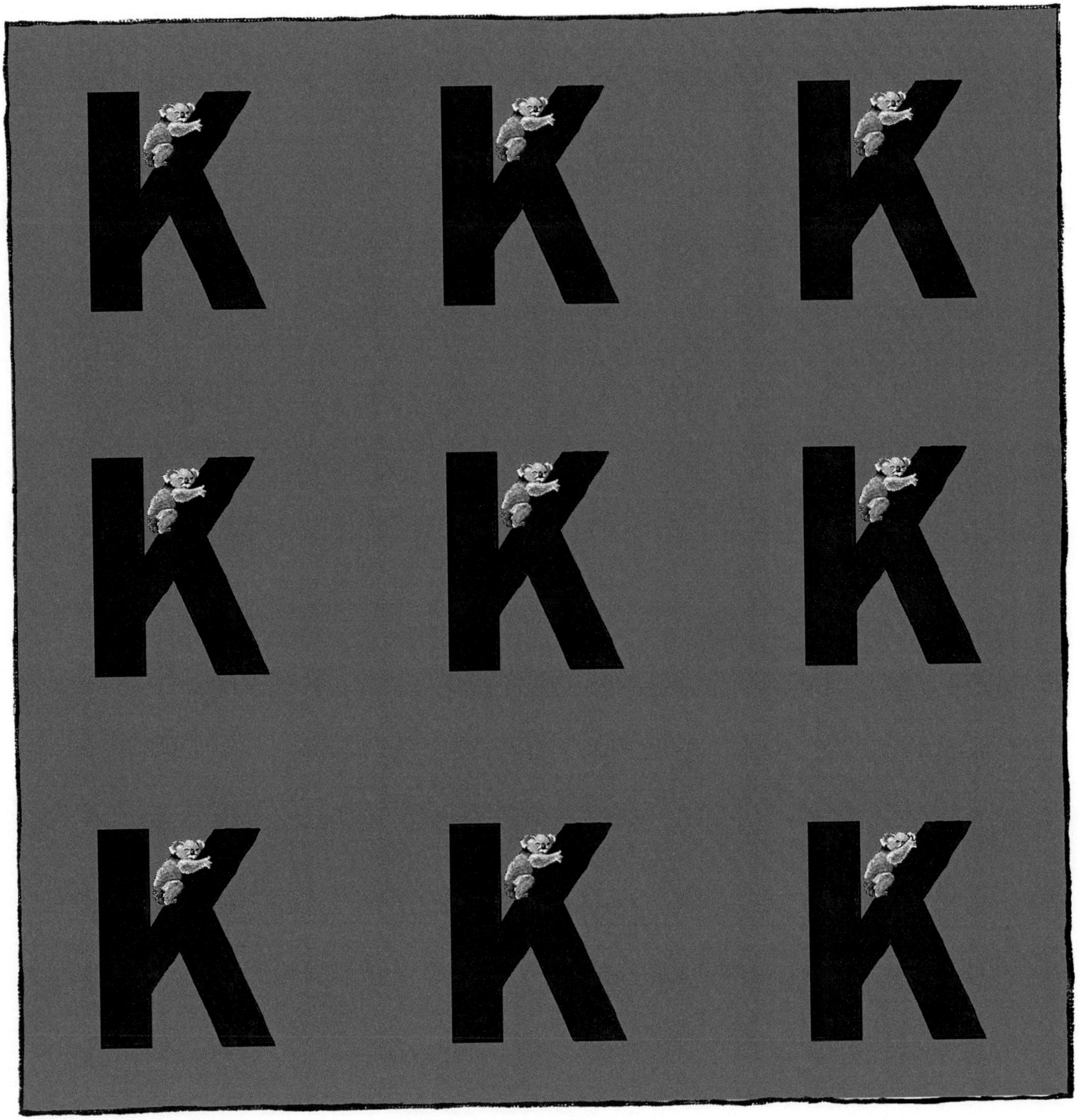
K K K
K K K
K K K

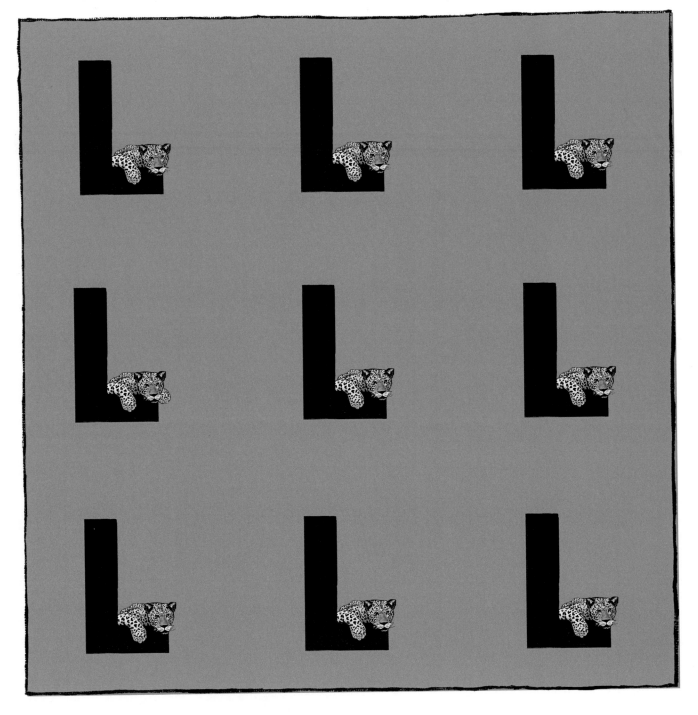

The lamb and the lion, the leopard and calf,
In peace in God's kingdom will dwell.
No creature will kill on God's holy hill.
All manner of things shall be well.

lamb   lion   leopard

The wolf shall dwell with the lamb, and the leopard shall lie down with the young goat, and the calf and the lion. **They shall not hurt or destroy in all my holy mountain; for the earth shall be full of the knowledge of the LORD as the waters cover the sea.** - Isaiah 11:6, 9

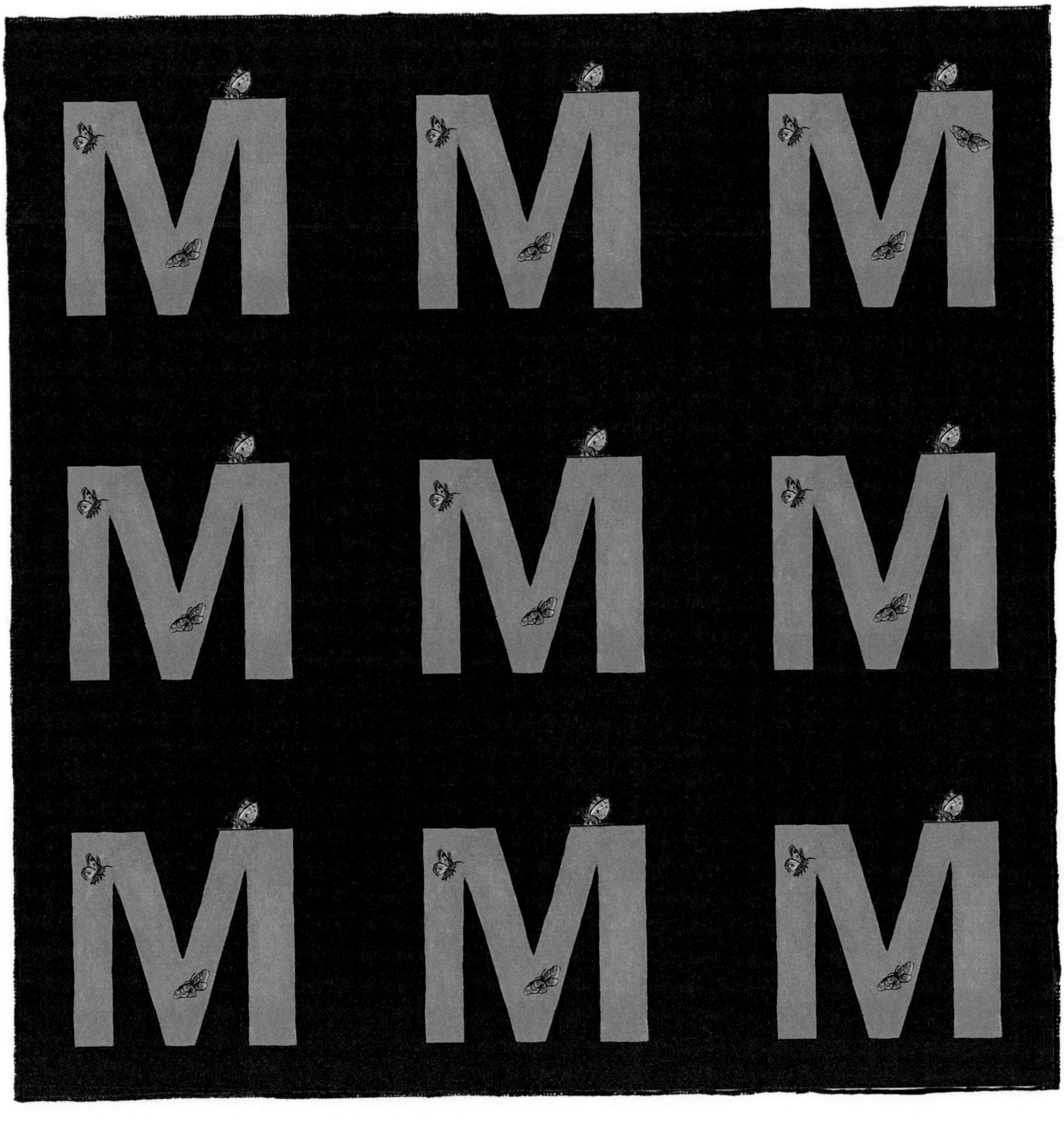
M M M
M M M
M M M

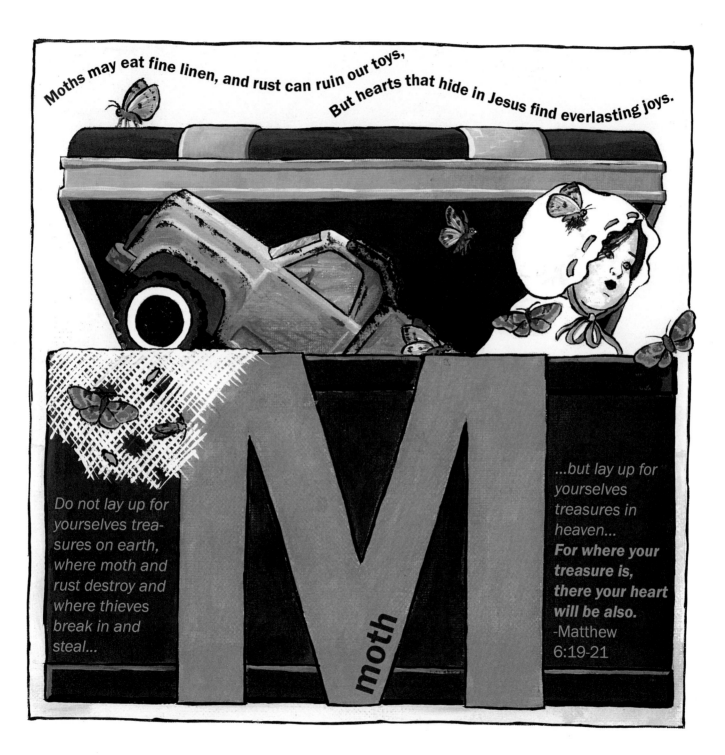

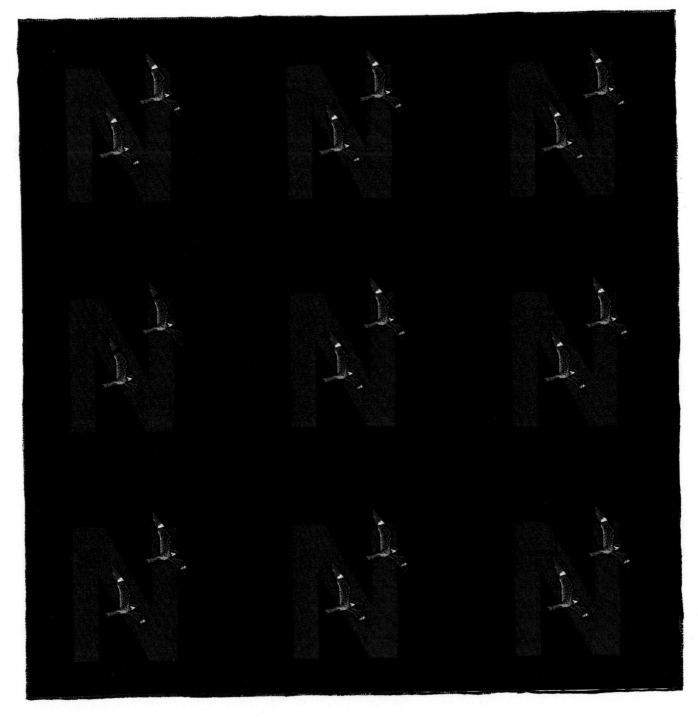

Night hawks, bats and vultures
God made off-bounds for food.
With every holy law
God sought His people's good.

night hawk

Among the birds, they shall not be eaten--
...the vulture... the nighthawk... the bat...
-Leviticus 11:13, 16, 19
The law of the LORD is perfect, reviving the soul. -Psalm 19:7

O owl in the desert,
Why do you cry?
Are you lonely, too?
Is this why you sigh?

Hear my prayer, O LORD;
Let my cry come to you!
I am like a desert owl
in the wilderness, like an
owl of the waste places.
-Psalm 102:1, 6

P P P

P P P

P P P

A **praying** mantis on a twig
Becomes a graphic word
That every breathing
creature
Should praise the living Lord.

praying mantis

Let everything that
has breath praise
the LORD!
-Psalm 150:6

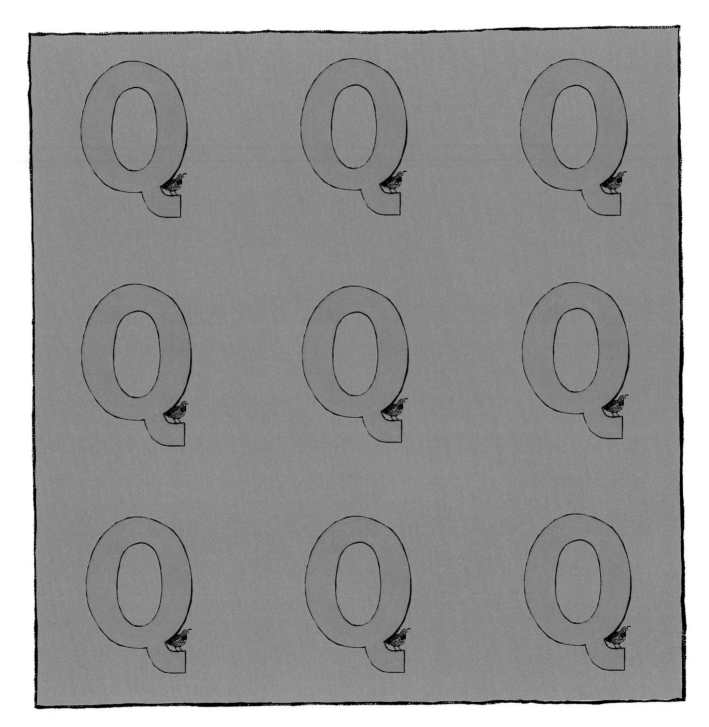

The quails that tumbled
from the sky,
With manna on the side,
Became the proof the
Hebrews craved:
The Lord God
will provide.

*At twilight you shall
eat meat, and in the
morning you shall be
filled with bread (manna).*
**Then you shall know that
I am the LORD your God.**
-Exodus 16:12

quail

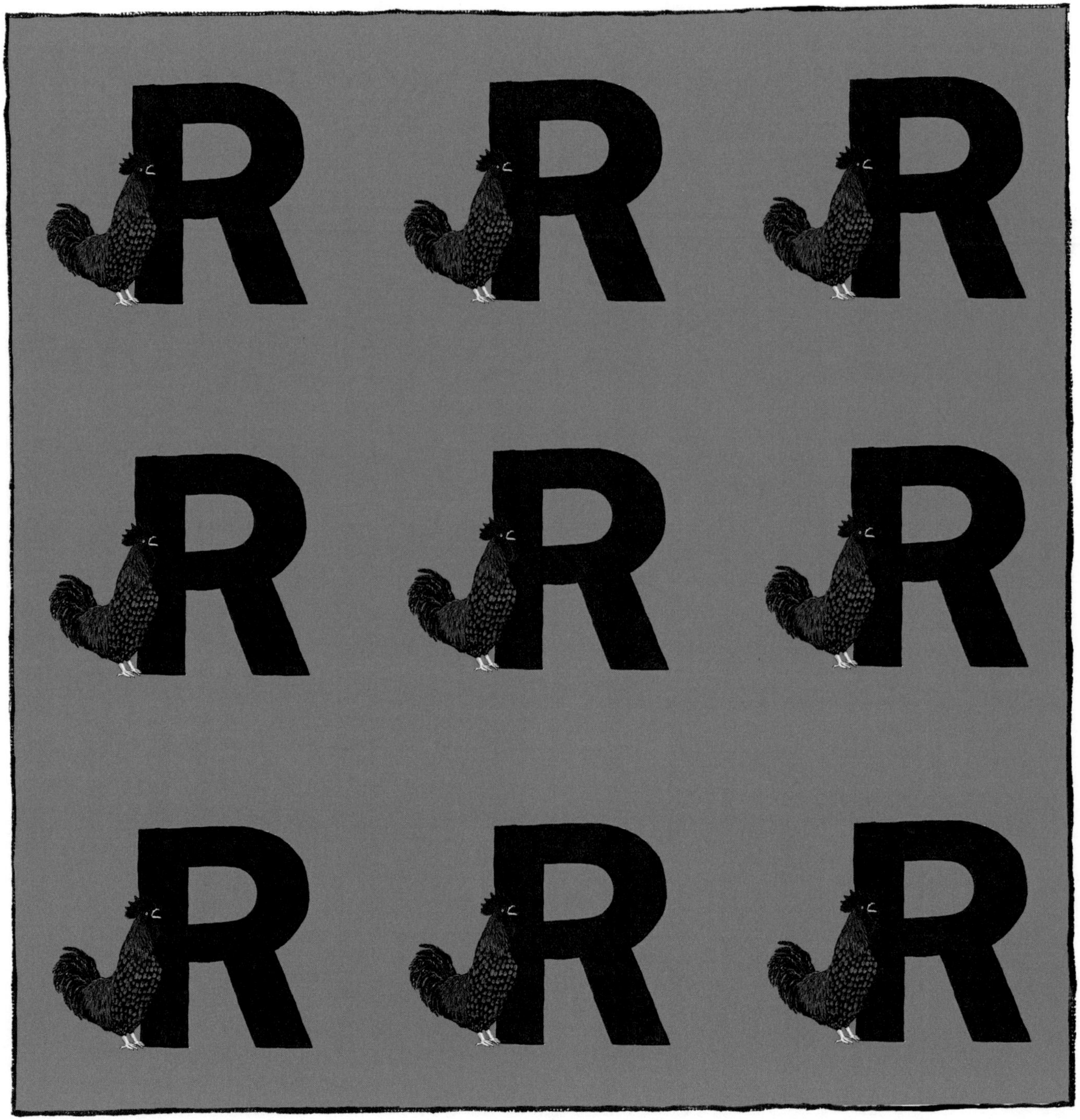
R R R
R R R
R R R

A **rooster** crowing far away
Brought shame to Peter's heart that day.
From fear his Master he denied,
"I don't know Jesus," Peter lied.

I do not know this man.
-Mark 14:71

rooster

Yet in the resurrection light
When Jesus saw he was contrite.
He came to Peter on the shore
To speak the words that would restore.

If we confess our sins, God is faithful
and just to forgive us our sins... -I John 1:9

Each time a
tiny sparrow falls,
The heavenly Father sees.
What reason then
have we to fear?
He loves us
more than these.

sparrow

And not one sparrow will fall to the ground apart from your Father...
Fear not, therefore; you are of more value than many sparrows. -Matthew 10:29, 31

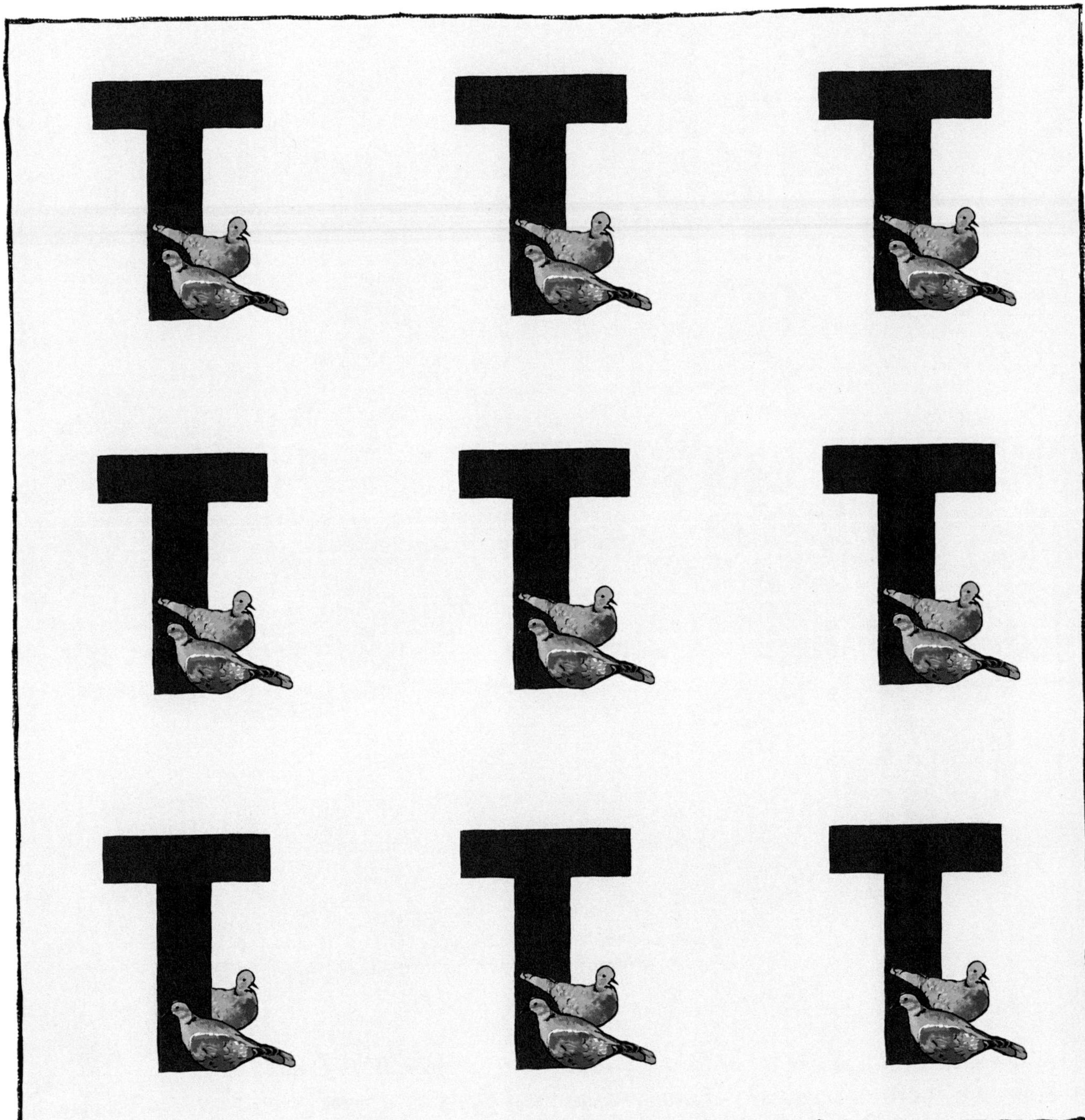
T T T
T T T
T T T

Two turtledoves to the temple they brought— Mary and Joseph in thanks for their son. Anna and Simeon joined them in praise, Knowing this baby was God's chosen One.

turtledove

They brought him up to Jerusalem to present him to the Lord... and to offer a sacrifice... of a pair of turtle-doves. -Luke 2:22, 24

Simeon took him up in his arms and blessed God and said, **'my eyes have seen your salvation.'** *-Luke 2:28, 30*

Anna began to give thanks to God and to speak of him to all who were waiting for the redemption of Jerusalem. -Luke 2:38

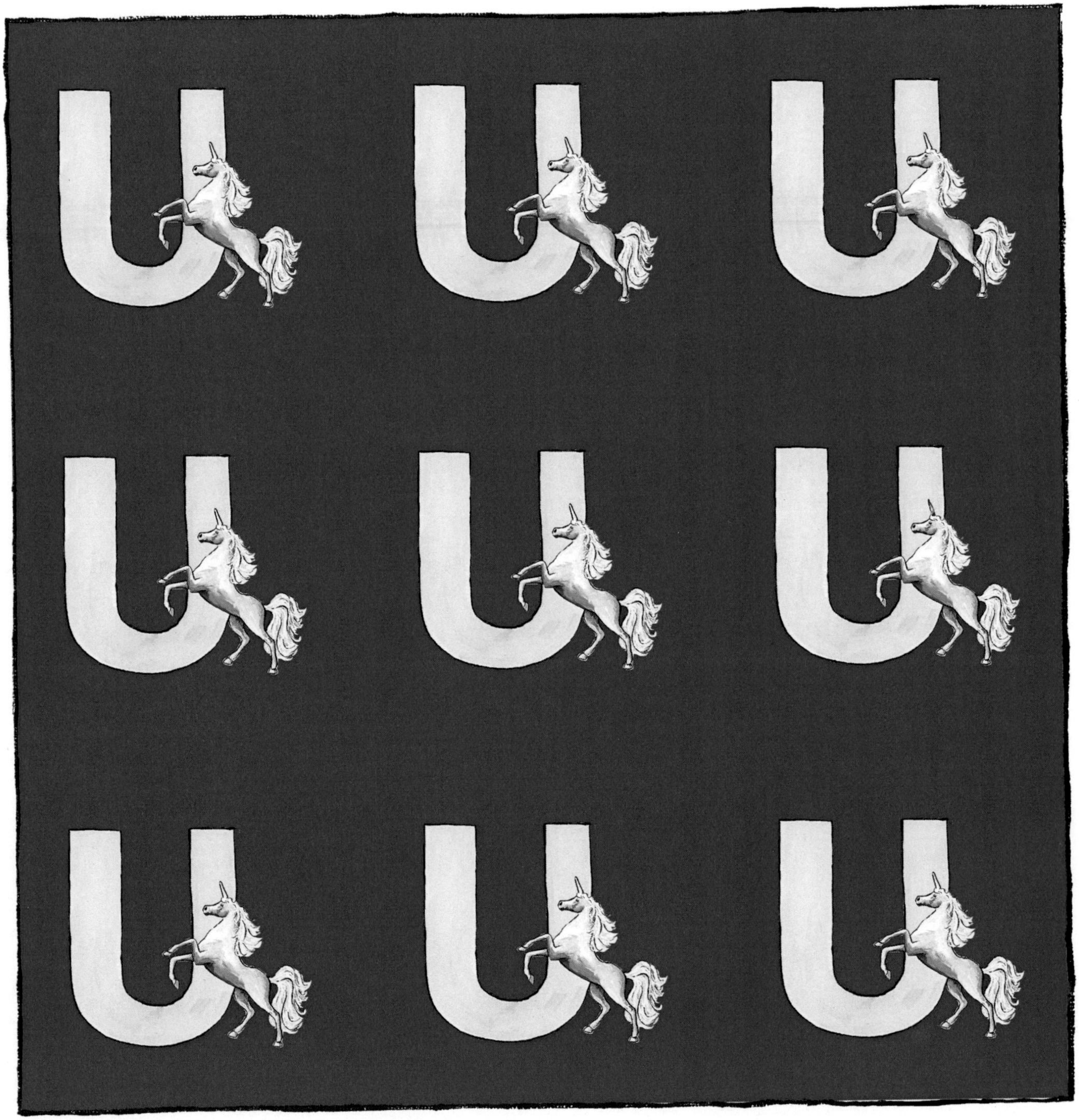

It may have been a **unicorn**
That God revealed to Job
To show His servant who was boss
Of all who walk the globe.

unicorn

U

Whatever is under the whole heaven is mine. -Job 41:11

Will the unicorn be willing to serve thee? -Job 39:9 KJV
Note: The English Standard Version says, "Is the wild ox willing to serve you?" But God's point is the same.

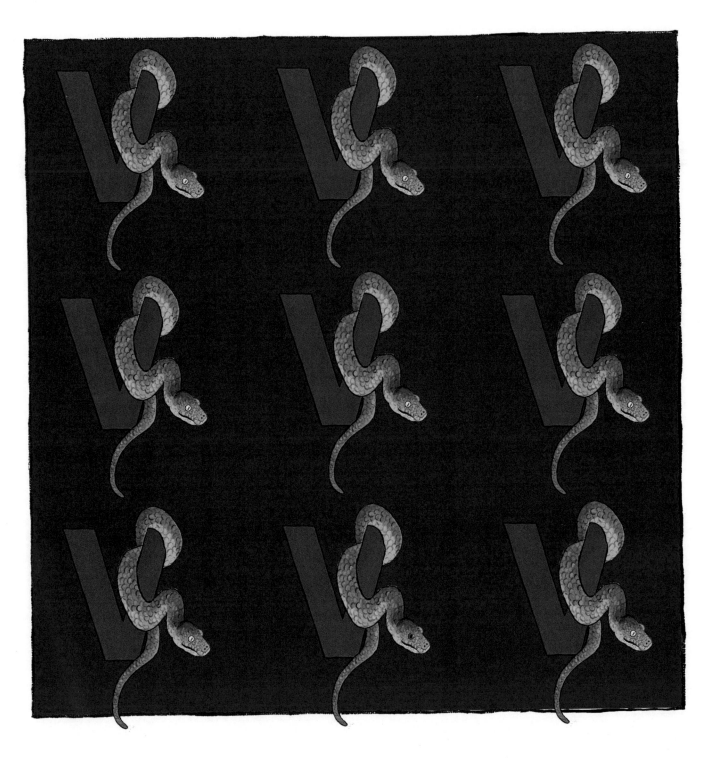

W W W

W W W

W W W

Wolves are on the prowl
for sheep,
So Jesus warns us to beware:
"Be meek as doves but wise
as snakes."
Only fools do not take care.

W

wolf

Behold, I am sending
you out as sheep in the
midst of wolves, so
**be wise as serpents
and innocent as doves.**
-Matthew 10:16

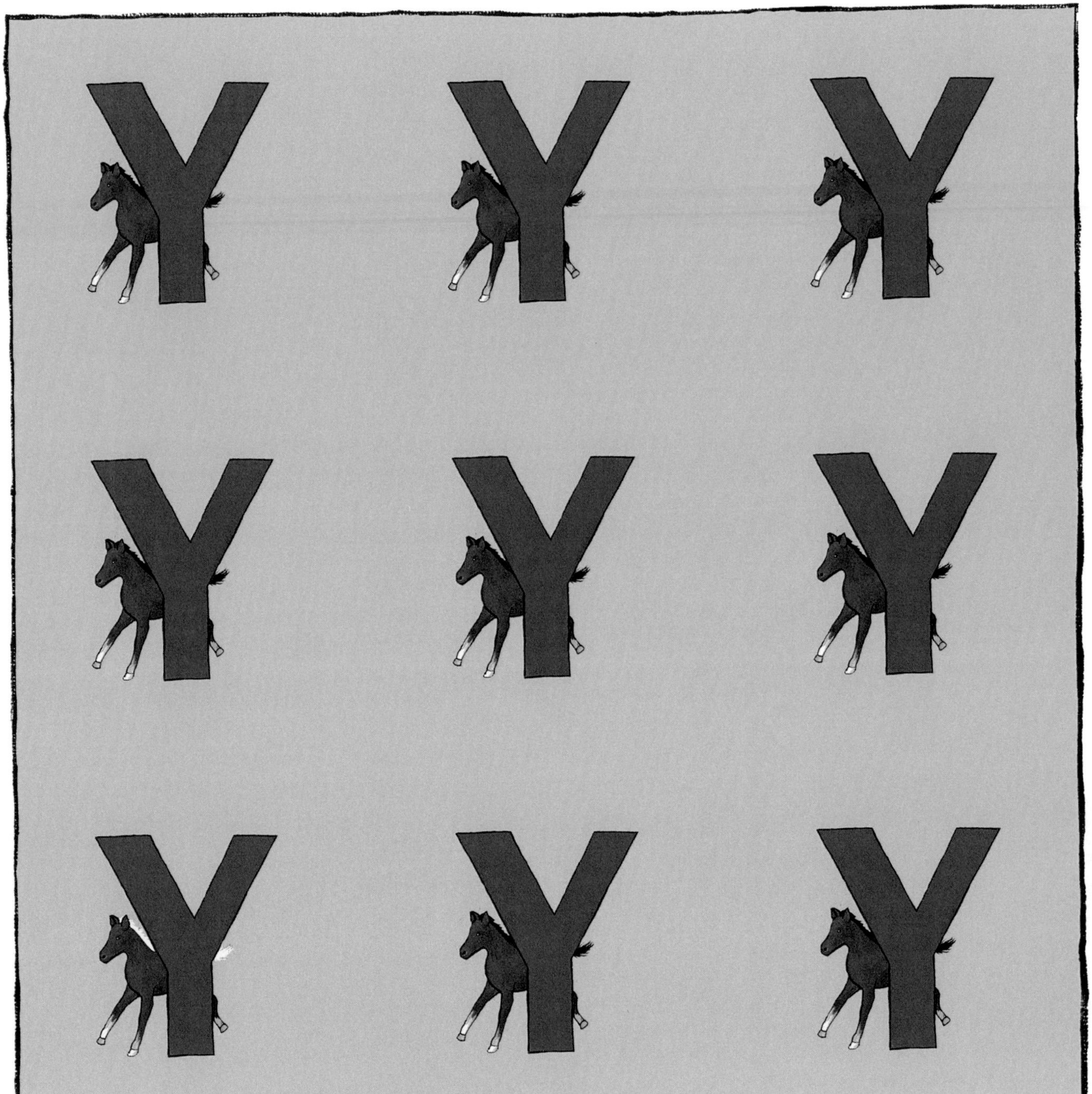
Y
Y
Y
Y
Y
Y
Y
Y
Y

Yearlings are young horses,
and horses were the key
For victory in warfare
before technology.

The Lord God gave His people
a better strategy:
Put not your trust in horses,
put all your trust in me.

*Some trust in chariots, and
some in horses, but we trust
in the name of the LORD our God.*
-Psalm 20:7

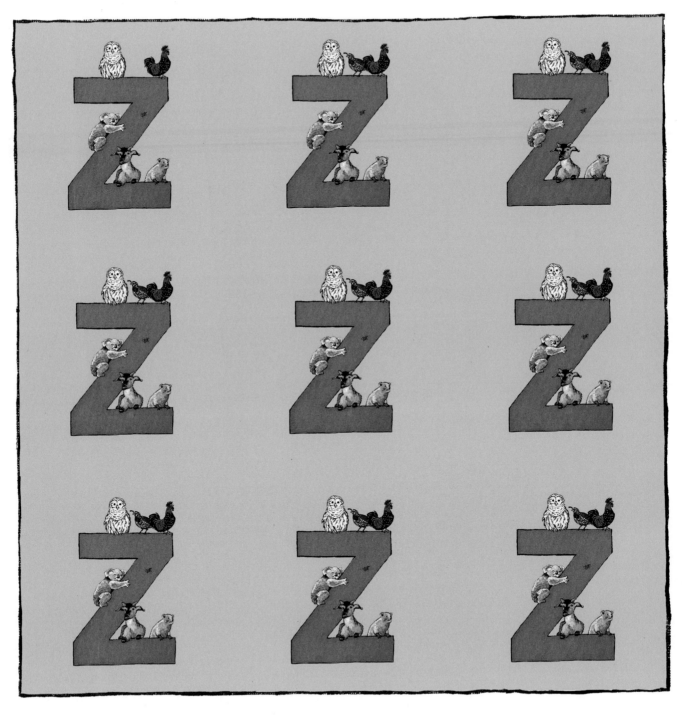

Since *Zoe's* the Greek word for "life,"
A zoo is one place we may see
The mammals, the insects and birds,
Whose names stretch from A down to Z.

"Very good" came the verdict of God
When His work of creation was done.
God granted this honor to Adam:
The privilege of naming each one.

And God saw everything that
he had made, and behold, it was
very good. -Genesis 1:31
Now out of the ground the LORD God had
formed every beast of the field and every bird
of the heavens and brought them to the man to see
what he would call them. And whatever the man called
every living creature, that was its name. -Genesis 2:19

Peggy & Cheryl

About the Author

Peggy Noll has loved books ever since her big sister taught her to read before she started kindergarten. She studied English Literature for a Master's Degree and taught Children's Literature at a community college. Her special joy, however, was reading to their five children and later seven grandchildren. After their children were grown, Peggy and her husband Steve, an Anglican priest and biblical scholar, became missionaries in Africa. During their ten years in Uganda, Peggy co-founded a children's library on the campus of Uganda Christian University, which has continued to thrive since they returned to the U.S. in 2010. It is no surprise that with this background and years of publishing occasional articles and stories as a freelance writer, she started writing alphabetical verses featuring animals in the Bible.

About the Illustrator

Cheryl DeGraaf began drawing and painting at an early age. She has painted murals on church nurseries, pediatrician offices and many play rooms to delight and amuse children. A graduate of Carnegie Mellon School of Design, she and her husband John have a lively home where their 8 children, a dog, a cat, and a hamster peacefully coexist. She enjoys homeschooling her children, and leading a homeschool co-op where she teaches art weekly. Although she makes her home north of Pittsburgh, she regularly takes trips out west with her family to explore the Rockies from Arizona to Alberta.

For Steve, my husband and chief encourager. And for our children, grandchildren, godchildren, and children everywhere, in the spirit of finding delight as well as truth and guidance for their lives in the best book of all- the Holy Bible!
P.N.

For my children, with gratitude for all your editing, critiques, brainstorming and enthusiastic encouragement of this project. May you always delight in the beauties and wonders of the creation, but most importantly, may you delight in our great God and Creator.
C.D.

Our thanks to Elizabeth for introducing us.

Giraffe & Vole Press • Text copyright ©2017 by Peggy Noll • Illustrations copyright ©2017 by Cheryl DeGraaf • All rights reserved, including the right of reproduction in whole or in part in any form (with the exception of short quotes for the purpose of review) • ISBN 9781976537516 • Unless otherwise noted, all Scripture quotations are from the ESV® Bible (The Holy Bible, English Standard Version®), copyright 2001 by Crossway, a publishing ministry of Good News Publishers. Used by permission. All rights reserved. • Printed in the United States of America.

Giraffe & Vole Press • GiraffeandVole.com

63867138R00033

Made in the USA
Middletown, DE
07 February 2018